AF334962

Oregon Territory

Oregon Territory

By

Aaron V. Brown

Ye Galleon Press

Fairfield, Washington

1967

AARON VENABLE BROWN

August 15, 1795 • March 8, 1859

THE author of this booklet was born in Brunswick County, Virginia, a son of the Reverend Aaron Brown, a Methodist minister and veteran of the Revolutionary War. Aaron V. Brown was the sixth child of the Rev. Brown and his second wife, Elizabeth Melton. He attended Westrayville Academy, North Carolina, and was graduated from the University of North Carolina in 1814, valedictorian of his class. He was admitted to the Tennessee bar in 1817, and later became a partner and life long friend of James K. Polk. Brown was a Tennessee state senator 1821 ⸱ 25 and a state representative, 1831 ⸱ 33. He was a member of the U.S. House of Representatives for the Twenty⸱sixth, the Twenty⸱seventh and the Twenty⸱eighth Congresses, March 4, 1839 to March 3, 1845, and was Governor of Tennessee, 1845 ⸱ 1847. He was appointed Post⸱master General by President James Buchanan, and served in this capacity from March 6, 1857 until his death in Washington, D.C., March 8, 1859. He was first married to Sarah Burruss by whom he had four children. Some time after her death he married Mrs. Cynthia (Pillow) Saunders, and by her had a son. He was an able administrator and was widely respected. He is buried at Mount Olivet cemetery in Nashville, Tennessee.

OREGON TERRITORY.

[To accompany bill H. R. No. 21.]

March 12, 1844.

Mr. A. V. Brown, from the Committee on the Territories, made the following

REPORT:

*The Committee on the Territories, to whom was referred the bill No. 21,
"to organize a Territorial Government in the Oregon Territory, and
for other purposes," beg leave to present the following report:*

The committee have not thought it advisable to recommend the passage
of the bill referred to them, organizing as it does a new and distinct Territorial Government for the Oregon country. They have considered the
present population of that region hardly sufficient for such a purpose. They
have, however, prepared another bill, in lieu of that one, which is herewith
reported, and its passage most earnestly recommended to the favorable consideration of the House. This bill proposes to extend the civil and crimi-
nal jurisdiction of the Territory of Iowa over all our Pacific and intermediate possessions. It provides for the establishment of the necessary military posts within the country, and on the principal route leading to it. It
pledges the future action of Congress in giving to all such as have gone, or
may go there, such an interest in land as may secure to them homes, and
some remuneration for the toils and hardships incident to the settlement of
every new country. Such provisions have been inserted in the proposed
amendment, as will make the exercise of jurisdiction and the enforcement
of our laws in that distant country neither difficult nor expensive. We do
not doubt, however, that the whole arrangement will be of but brief dura-
tion; giving way, in a few years, to a full and complete organization of one
or more distinct Territorial Governments west of the Rocky mountains.

In presenting this bill thus modified, and recommending its passage, it is a
source of satisfaction to the committee to know that it is in precise accordance with the avowed opinions not only of the present, but of several pre-
ceding Presidents of the United States. As far back as December, 1824,
Mr. Monroe, in his annual message to the two Houses of Congress, strongly
recommended the propriety of establishing a military post at the mouth of
the Columbia river, or at some other point within our acknowledged limits.
This he did, not only as a protection to our then increasing commerce, and
to our fisheries, but as a protection to all our interests in that quarter, and
as a means of conciliating the various tribes of Indians throughout our
northwestern possessions. He further added, "that it was thought, also
that by the establishment of such a post, the *intercourse* between our western States and Territories and the Pacific, and our trade with the tribes

residing in the interior, on each side of the Rocky mountains, would be essentially promoted." Mr. Adams, in his message to the next succeeding Congress, follows up this suggestion of Mr. Monroe, and recommends not only the establishment of a military post at or near the mouth of the Columbia, but the equipment of a public ship for the exploration of the whole northwestern coast of this continent. If these recommendations are limited to the protection of our commerce and fisheries, to the trade with the intermediate Indian tribes, and to the promotion of our intercourse with the Pacific, it must have been only because at that time we had no fixed population there, looking to the permanent settlement of the country for agricultural purposes. Since 1824 and 1825, however, we have advanced far beyond the then necessities of our people, and are now called upon to give the protection of our laws and the benefit of our free institutions to those who have made it their permanent abode, and whose purposes are to bring into cultivation that vast portion of our empire.

The President of the United States, in his annual message at the commencement of the present session, presented these altered circumstances in the condition of that country to the attention of Congress, and with much cogency recommended the very measure which the committee have reported. He says: "In the mean time, it is proper to remark, that many of our citizens are either already established in the territory, or are on their way thither, for the purpose of forming permanent settlements, while others are preparing to follow; and, in view of these facts, I must repeat the recommendations contained in previous messages, for the establishment of military posts at such places on the line of travel, as will furnish security and protection to our hardy adventurers against hostile tribes of Indians inhabiting those extensive regions. Our laws should also follow them, so modified as the circumstances of the case may seem to require. Under the influence of our free system of government, new republics are destined to spring up, at no distant day, on the shores of the Pacific, similar in policy and in feeling to those existing on this side of the Rocky mountains, and giving a wider and more extensive spread to the principles of civil and religious liberty."

In the bill which we have reported, it will be found that we have responded not only to the opinions of Mr. Monroe and Mr. Adams in relation to the establishment of military posts, but we have adopted the just and proper sentiments of the present Executive in reference to the increased settlement of our population in that distant region. Our people have gone to Oregon, and we are only sending our laws after them. It might be greater precision, however, to say that our laws had *preceded* them; that they had been always there, coeval with our rights to the country; and that we are now only proposing to give them activity and force by government organization. In doing so, we introduce no new policy into the action of the Federal Government. At the time of the establishment of our national independence, our population was confined to a comparatively narrow slip of country bordering on the Atlantic. As fast, however, as our settlements extended into the west in sufficient numbers, new territories were established. These, at first, were confined to the Mississippi river for their common western boundary. After the acquisition of Louisiana, the same wise and necessary policy has been pursued, observing limits, in several cases, but little short of the Rocky mountains. In the rapid march of our empire-republic, the time has now arrived for the extension of the same policy beyond those mountains, recognising the shores of the Pacific as the only final terminus of our dominions.

The propriety of this extension is dependent, of course, on the validity of the title of the United States to the territory embraced in the bill. This question we were obliged to meet, anterior to all action on the subject. In its investigation, we have looked into the most authentic histories of voyages and discoveries on the northwestern coast of America. We have consulted the opinions of our most distinguished and best-informed public men, from Mr. Jefferson down to the present time. We have carefully examined all the treaties among the several nations claiming to have an interest in the subject; not neglecting to profit by the reports made by Mr. Baylies to the 19th, and Mr. Cushing to the 25th Congress, and by the several reports and speeches of the late lamented Senator from Missouri, who had devoted so much of the labor of his great mind to the investigation of this subject. The result of all this investigation has been a thorough conviction that the United States has a good and indefeasible title, as against any foreign power, to the country extending east and west from the Rocky mountains to the Pacific ocean; and north and south from the limits of Mexico, in latitude 42 degrees north, to those of Russia, in latitude 54 degrees 40 minutes north.

The southern boundary was fixed by the treaty with Spain in 1819, commonly called the Florida treaty. By that treaty, it is agreed that the boundary-line between the possessions of the two nations west of the Mississippi, after reaching the river Arkansas, shall be, " following the course of the southern bank of the Arkansas to its source in latitude 42 degrees ; and thence, by that parallel of latitude, to the South sea." In 1828 this line was confirmed by Mexico, as the successor of Spain, in a treaty of limits between herself and the United States.' The southern boundary, is then, fixed and certain. As to the northern one, it was settled at 54 degrees and 40 minutes by a treaty between the United States and Russia, dated 17th April, 1824; by which it was agreed that there should not be formed, by the citizens of the United States, or under the authority of the same, any establishment upon the northwest coast of America, nor in any of the islands adjacent, to the north of 54 degrees and 40 minutes of north latitude; and, in like manner, none by Russia or her subjects south of the same parallel of latitude.

By virtue of these treaties, Russia on the north, Mexico on the south, and the United States on the east, are all agreed and well satisfied as to the boundaries of the Oregon country. Great Britain alone asserts or pretends any title to it, or any part of it, adverse to that of the United States.

Before we enter upon any examination of her title, we respectfully beg leave to submit our views on another question presented to our consideration. It is contended that the passage of the bill now reported would be inconsistent with the actual relations of the two Governments defined by the convention of the 20th October, 1818. The 3d article is as follows:

" ART. 3. It is agreed that any country that may be claimed by either party on the northwest coast of America, westward of the Stony mountains, shall, together with its harbors, bays, and creeks, and the navigation of all rivers within the same, be free and open for the term of ten years from the date of the signature of the present convention, to the vessels, citizens, and subjects of the two powers. It being well understood, that this agreement is not to be construed to the prejudice of any claim which either of the two high contracting parties may have to any part of said country; nor shall it be taken to affect the claim of any other power or state to any part of said country: the only object of the high contracting parties, in that respect, being to prevent disputes and differences among themselves."

The provisions of this article were indefinitely extended by the convention of 1827—with, however, an agreement that it should be competent for either, at any time after the 20th of October, 1828, on giving due notice of twelve months to the other contracting party, to annul and abrogate said convention. The first remark which the committee will submit on the provisions of the 3d article of the convention of 1818, is, that they do not refer to the *possession* of the territory at all. That *possession* had always been in the United States until the war of 1812. It was then lost by conquest; but it was fully restored by the treaty of peace, and the formal surrender of it to the United States under that treaty. It was only the right of entering into the country—into its bays and harbors—for the mere purposes of such trade and commerce as was then carried on in that region, that was secured to the subjects of Great Britain. The same rights might have been extended to any of the ports, bays, and rivers of the Atlantic; but if extended in the precise words of the convention of 1818, who would have thought that Great Britain would have been admitted to the joint *occupancy* of Massachusetts, New York, Virginia, the Carolinas, and the other States of the Union?

If the possession of the territory was in the United States at the time of the convention of 1818—a fact which no one has ever attempted to deny—the provision of the 3d section can only be regarded as a permission to the subjects of Great Britain to participate with ours in the individual rights of trade and commerce enjoyed by our own citizens within the territory. The bill which is now reported does not eject them from the country-at all. It does not deprive them of the privilege of entering into the country, its bays and rivers;—not at all. But it even guaranties a fuller and more perfect enjoyment of these individual rights, under an organized and well-administered system of laws. From extreme caution, and to exhibit toward Great Britain the most scrupulous regard for all existing stipulations, which might be supposed to have an application to the subject, the bill proposes a speedy surrender of all British subjects who may be charged with any violations of our laws to the nearest British authorities having jurisdiction over such cases. The permission given to British subjects to participate with our own citizens in the enjoyment of personal or individual rights within the territory, never can be considered as circumscribing the right of the United States to establish a proper government for the regulation of all persons inhabiting the country, of which she had the undisputed possession. In this view, the provision for delivering up British subjects to their nearest tribunals could not have been justly required; but the same has been conceded by the committee, on the scrupulous principle just adverted to.

As to the twelve months' notice required to be given by the convention of 1827, the committee do not regard that as at all necessary, in order to open the way to such action as is contemplated by this bill. The committee do not know that, for the purpose of organizing such a government as is now contemplated, it is at all important to annul or abrogate that convention. That country is large, and there is evidently room enough for the subjects and citizens of both countries, in the exercise of all their enterprise in trade and commerce. All that will be required of them is to conform to the laws, and to respect the institutions, which we may establish. Doing this, we shall

never envy the equal participation in the benefits and advantages to be derived from a well organized system of government. Any possible incon-
veniences arising from the continuance of the convention of 1827, not now
anticipated by the committee, can, and doubtless will, be looked to by the
Executive, who can at any time abrogate the same, by giving the notice
contemplated in it. The giving of that notice, being a matter of treaty stipulation, belongs, perhaps, exclusively to the Executive; on whose province
there is no occasion, and the committee have no inclination, to intrude.

In connexion with this branch of the subject, the committee will advert
to the fact, (as it is now understood to be,) that negotiations are in progress
between the United States and Great Britain on the subject of this territory.
They conceive that this should make no difference in the action of the
committee. They have to act on the subject as it is *now* presented to them—
not as it *may be* changed or altered hereafter, by any future arrangements
between the two countries. If the United States have *now* the right to the
Oregon country—if they have *now* the sole and undisputed possession of
it—if our people have *now* permanent settlements in it, and are every day
suffering for the want of a properly-organized government to protect the
virtuous and to restrain the vicious,—we ought not to withhold our action,
under the possibility of some alteration in the relations of the two countries
in that region, at some uncertain and indefinite period. That negotiation
can still progress; and any treaty stipulation inconsistent with our legislation, will control it to the extent of such interference. No one, we believe, supposes that the pending negotiations can ever result in the entire
loss of the Oregon country. Enough will doubtless remain of it, under
any circumstances, to require the extension of our laws in the manner now
contemplated. If the present negotiation relates (as the committee appre-
hend it does) solely to the ascertainment and settlement of the northern
boundary of the territory, they can anticipate, from no examination which
they have been able to make, any such loss of country in that direction, as
will at all affect the propriety of the passage of the bill which is now presented to the House.

There is enough, doubtless, for that negotiation to act upon, without re-
sorting even to the supposition that any portion of our territory south of latitude 54 degrees 40 minutes north may be lost. We propose the extension
of our laws fully up to that latitude, and will now submit the grounds on
which we maintain that the United States has a full and indefeasible right
and title to that point. We adopt as our own, and submit to the House, the
views of a former committee* on the question of title; which we believe
must carry conviction to every disinterested and impartial mind:

As preliminary to the discussion of the contested points of the case, and
as needful to the full understanding of its merits, the committee premise a
brief account of the voyages of discovery, enterprises, and settlements of
the powers in question, on the northwest coast and interior of the continent, so far as they bear upon the present controversy; referring to the doc-
uments appended to this report for a full and detailed account of the history of northwestern discovery.

Spain, having established her power in Mexico, was impelled, by the same
causes which led to the original conquest, to seek its extension. She was impelled to undertake expeditions by sea and land to the northwest, by another
inducement—namely, the hope of discovering a direct northerly passage, by

---

* See Mr. Cushing's report to the 25th Congress.

sea, from the Atlantic to the Pacific ocean ; which anticipated passage used to be projected in the old maps of the seventeenth century by the name of the Straits of Anian.

Hernan Cortes himself set the example of these enterprises, by undertaking several of them at his own charge, and conducting one of them in person, exploring the Gulf of California, and thus leading the way to the settlement of that country, and to the subsequent voyages of the Spaniards and others along the northwestern coast of America. Prior to the visit of any other European power, the Spaniards had prosecuted their discoveries to Cape Mendocin and Cape Blanco, in voyages of unquestionable authenticity. Complete and authentic evidence also exists, that Don Esteban Martinez, in 1774, made the first discovery of the sound of Nootka ; that in 1775 Don Bruno Heceta, Don Juan de Ayala, and Don Juan de la Bodega y Quadra, were the first to discover the bay of the river Columbia, which they called *Entrada de Heceta.*

Though there is not the same authentic evidence of some other voyages of ancient date in that quarter ascribed to Spanish navigators, yet it is at present generally admitted that in 1599 Juan de Fuca discovered and explored the strait which now universally bears his name.

The river Columbia itself was first entered and explored by Captain Robert Gray, of Boston, in the year 1792, in the ship Columbia. whose name, applied to the river, also perpetuates the memory of the original discovery.

The first European establishment founded on any part of the northwest coast, from California to the 49th degree of north latitude, was made by Fidalgo, in 1799, on the main land at the entrance of the strait of Juan de Fuca.

Leaving the Pacific, we find that three only of the great European powers acquired a permanent foothold in North America, from the side of the Atlantic.

Spain secured to herself the countries of Mexico extending from the Gulf of Mexico to the Pacific, and so indefinitely to the northwest ; and also the country of Florida, limited to the northeastern shore of the Gulf.

France obtained the valley of the St. Lawrence on the one hand, and that of the Mississippi on the other ; the whole connected together by the great lakes, and constituting a noble and unique territory, stretching from the northeast to the southwest, in the rear of the English settlements on the Atlantic, restricted by them on the east, but extending westward indefi-nitely towards the Pacific and the possessions of Spain.

England got possession of the region of country on the Atlantic, extending from the neighborhood of the St. Lawrence on the northeast, to Florida on the south, and westward indefinitely, in conflict with the claims of France in that direction. England also established herself in the waters of Hudson's bay, with a claim extending into the interior indefinitely, in conflict with the claims of France along the St. Lawrence and the great lakes

Whatever rights, be the same more or less, were held by Spain in the northwest, have, as already stated, been expressly ceded to the United States by Spain and by the Mexican republic.

Whatever rights Great Britain had in virtue of her possessions between the St. Lawrence and Florida, she recognised as vested in the United States by the treaty concluded at Paris the 3d September, 1783, commonly called the " treaty of peace ;" acknowledging the said States to be free, sovereign, and independent; and relinquishing "all claims to the government, propriety, *and territorial rights of the same, and every part thereof.*"

Whatever rights France had, subsequently to the conquest by Great Britain and the now United States, (for *we* performed a large part of that work,) of that part of her possessions lying on the St. Lawrence, she ceded to the United States, by the treaty concluded at Paris the 30th of April, 1803, commonly called "the Louisiana treaty."

At the date of the Florida treaty, therefore, in 1819, there remained to Great Britain, of her ancient territory in North America, only the countries of the St. Lawrence and of Hudson's bay; all the residue of the continent, eastward of the Rocky mountains, and south and west to the confines of the Mexican republic, having become undeniably vested in the United States.

This result was reached by various treaties and conventions between Spain, France, Great Britain, and the United States; the combination of which treaties restricted or extended, in one way or another, by express compacts, the respective territories of Great Britain and the United States; which compacts, therefore, and the acts consequent on them, constitute the next stage in the history of the title of the United States to the territory of Oregon.

By treaty between Great Britain and France, concluded at Utrecht, the 17th of April, 1713, art. iii, "Hudson's bay, together with all lands, &c., which belong thereunto," was restored to Great Britain; and the article proceeds :

"It is agreed on both sides to determine within a year, by commissioners to be forthwith named by each party, the limits which are to be fixed between the said Bay of Hudson and the places appertaining to the French; * * * * the same commissioners shall also have orders to describe and settle, in like manner, the boundaries between the other British and French colonies in those parts."—*Jenkinson's Treaties*, vol. 2.

And the commissioners appointed under this article adopted the 49th parallel of latitude as the line of demarcation between the possessions of England and France in that quarter, and west of the Mississippi; in pursuance of which, the same limit was ratified and confirmed between Great Britain and the United States, as the successor of France, by the second article of the convention of the 20th of October, 1818, so far west as to the Rocky mountains.

By the treaty between Great Britain, France, and Spain, concluded at Paris the 10th of February, 1763, the former was confirmed in the possession of the conquered provinces of France on the St. Lawrence; and, on the other hand, relinquished irrevocably all claims to territory beyond the Mississippi, in the seventh article, as follows:

"The confines between the British and French possessions in North America shall be fixed irrevocably (seront irrévocablement fixés) by a line drawn along the middle of the Mississippi, from its source to the river Iberville; and from thence, by the middle of the river Iberville, and the lakes Maurepas and Pontchartrain, to the sea;" (that is, to the Gulf of Mexico.)—(*Chalmers*, vol. ii; *Martens Recueil*, vol. 1.)

The Louisiana treaty cedes to the United States the colony or province of Louisiana, with the same extent it had in the hands of Spain in 1800, and that it had when previously possessed by France, with all its rights and appurtenances.

This description is, to be sure, sufficiently loose. But Napoleon, having made the cession at the moment of going to war with Great Britain, and having made it to prevent the country from falling into the hands of the latter, and having ceded it to the United States out of friendly feelings towards us, and in order to augment our power as against that of Britain ;—being actuated by these motives, he, of course, chose to execute a quitclaim, rather than a warranty of boundaries; and the United States, placed in the position of acquiring, at a cheap price, a territory of a value altogether inestimable to her, (for Louisiana would have been well purchased at a cost of twenty times sixty millions of francs,) had no disposition to be hypercritical on this point, and thus hazard the loss of such a favorable contingency. (*Barbē Marbois, Hist. &c. de la Louisiane.*) And though much controversy sprang up in regard to the southwestern or southeastern limits of Louisiana, yet all this resolved itself at length into a question with Spain, as did also the doubts as to the western limits of Louisiana.

Mr. Jefferson, at any rate, took enlarged views of the rights of the United States in this respect; and in his message to Congress of the 18th of January, 1803, recommended the exploration of the northwestern parts of the country—not on the Missouri merely, but "even to the Western ocean;" putting the expediency as well as constitutionality of the exploration expressly on the ground of its being territory claimed by the United States ; and the fruit of this recommendation was the celebrated expedition of Lewis and Clark.

Prior to that time, little was known of the vast region watered by the Missouri and the Columbia, and of the intervening Rocky mountains, now so familiar to the hardy hunters of the west. Of the latter river, the earliest mention known to the committee is by Jonathan Carver, a citizen of the then colony of Connecticut, who travelled among the Indians of the Upper Mississippi in 1763, and who, in his book, speaks of the "Oregon, or River of the West," and of "the river Oregon, or River of the West, that falls into the Pacific ocean at the straits of Anian." It is probable that Carver derived his idea of the existence of this river from the wandering Indians, among whom he lived, and who had either crossed the Rocky mountains themselves, or received visits from the Indians on the other side. This, at all events, seems to be the origin of the name OREGON. For there is no account of the inlet of the river Columbia having been seen by European Christians prior to Heceta's voyage in 1775 ; or the mouth of the river, before the time of Robert Gray in 1792 ; or its upper waters, until the expedition of Lewis and Clark. Thirty years after the travels of Carver, indeed, Alexander Mackenzie crossed the Rocky mountains in the extreme north, and fell upon a river which he supposed to be the Columbia ; but it is now well known and admitted on all hands that he was mistaken, and that the river he saw is no part of the Columbia. So that, whilst Americans were the first to navigate the river Columbia upwards from its mouth, so were they also the first to explore it downwards from its sources. Lewis and Clark not only explored the country as ours, but they took possession in behalf of the United States; and the expedition itself, the published account of which went forth to the world, was notice to all nations of our claim of title, and of the possession, by the erection of works and otherwise in assertion of the title.

This expedition was speedily followed by the actual occupation of the mouth of the river for the purposes of trade and settlement, with the sanction of the United States. In 1811, John Jacob Astor, of New York, (who, by his successful competition with British fur companies in the northwest, had already been of essential service to the United States in neutralizing to some degree the hostile influence exercised by foreign traders over the Indians of the United States,) foresaw the ultimate political importance of the Columbia, and conceived the noble idea of carrying his enterprises beyond the Rocky mountains, and establishing a factory as the nucleus of a future settlement and colonization of the Oregon. The classic narrative of this magnificent undertaking, by Washington Irving, has spread the fame of Mr. Astor's great design wherever the English language is read.

The establishment at Astoria was anterior to that of any other power on the Columbia. It was broken up in 1812, fraudulently sold to the Northwest Company by one of Mr. Astor's agents, and taken possession of by the British as an act of war. But the United States claimed that *the sale* to the Northwest Company of course did not affect the national jurisdiction, which continued of right in the United States ; and that, in obedience to the 1st article of the treaty of Ghent, which stipulated for the mutual restitution of "all territory, places, and possession whatsoever, taken by either party from the other during the war," Astoria (or Fort George) should be restored to the United States ; and it was done in 1818, in the most formal manner. Mr. Prevost proceeded thither from Lima, and received the surrender, as agent of the United States, in the following terms :

"Act of surrender and acknowledgment.

" In obedience to the commands of his Royal Highness the Prince Regent, signified in a despatch from the right honorable Earl Bathurst, addressed to the partners or agents of the Northwest Company, bearing date 27th January, 1818, and in obedience to subsequent orders, dated 26th July last, from William H. Sheriff, esq., captain of his Majesty's ship Andromache, we, the undersigned, do, in conformity to the 1st article of the treaty of Ghent, restore to the Government of the United States, through its agent, J. B. Prevost, esq., the settlement of Fort George, on the river Columbia.

" Given under our hands, in triplicate, at Fort George, Columbia river, this 6th of October, 1818.

" F. HICKEY,
" *Captain of his Majesty's ship Blossom.*
" JAMES KEITH,
" *Of the Northwest Company.*"

It is true, that in the despatch of Earl Bathurst, and in Lord Castlereagh's instructions to the British minister at Washington, a reservation is made, that the surrender of possession should not be deemed an admission of the absolute and exclusive right of dominion claimed by the United States ; but at the same time, in explanation to Mr. Rush, as stated in a published despatch, "Lord Castlereagh *admitted, in the most ample extent, our right to be reinstated, and to be the party in possession while treating of the title.*" In this condition were the rights of the parties in 1818, at the time of the signature of the convention of the 20th of October ; and by virtue of the express stipulations of that convention, in the same condition (so far as regards possession) do the rights of the parties still continue. If our title was good then, it is good now ; and whatever defects, if any, there were in it then, have been healed by the Florida treaty ; and by the direct admissions of the British Government, *we are entitled now to be in possession of the territory, and so to remain, until the question of ultimate title can be determined.*

It would seem, indeed, that the English themselves are beginning to entertain rational views on the subject ; for, in remarking upon it recently, a respectable London journal (the Post) says :

" The United States Government now says that the agent of the American Fur Company had no right to dispose of the jurisdiction ; and the President, it would appear, is determined to enforce that claim. It must be admitted that the United States have apparently a good case ; and if, on investigation, it be found that the sale of the property only took place, and that the allegiance could not be transferred, the surrender of the post to the United S ates may be the most prudent course. We have but a limited interest in the occupation of Astoria, while to the United States it is of great importance."

Having thus detailed the general facts affecting the title, it now becomes the duty of the committee to resume these facts, and to apply to them the recognised principles of the law of nations, which prescribe the rights of the parties.

The civilized people of Europe and America, which are associated together by their identity of origin and religion, and still more by the innumerable ties of a common civilization, of commercial and social intercourse, and the intercommunication of arts and of knowledge, and which recognise a rule of mutual dealing, composed of treaty stipulations, of prescriptive usages, and of certain general principles of right, called the law of nations,—these people have been accustomed to acquire and to define their possessions in America by the rule of—1. The right of discovery and exploration, followed by settlement ; and, 2. Its corollary, the right of extension by contiguity to actual settlements.

This rule, in its elementary ingredients, is thus laid down by Vattel :

" All mankind have an equal right to things that have not yet fallen into the possession of any one ; and those things belong to the person who first takes possession of them. When, therefore, a nation finds a country uninhabited, and without an owner, it may lawfully take possession of it ; and after it has sufficiently made known its will in this respect, it cannot be deprived of it by another nation. Thus, navigators going on voyages of discovery, furnished with a commission from their sovereign, and meeting with islands or other lands in a desert state, have taken possession of them in the name of their nation ; and this title has been usually respected, provided it was soon after followed by a real possession."—(§ 207, Chitty's Vattel.)

" The whole earth is destined to feed its inhabitants ; but this it would be incapable of doing if it were uncultivated. Every nation is then obliged, by the law of nature, to cultivate the land that has fallen to its share ; and it has no right to enlarge its boundaries, or have recourse to the assistance of other nations, but in proportion as the land in its possession is incapable of furnishing it with necessaries. Those nations (such as the ancient Germans, and some modern Tartars) who inhabit fertile countries, but disdain to cultivate their lands, and choose rather to live by plunder, are wanting to themselves, are injurious to all their neighbors, and deserve to be extirpated as savage and pernicious beasts. There are others, who, to avoid labor, choose to live only by hunting, and their flocks. This might, doubtless, be allowed in the first ages of the world, when the earth, without cultivation, produced more than was sufficient to feed its small number of inhabitants. But at present, when the human race is so greatly multiplied, it could not subsist if all nations were disposed to live in that manner. Those who still pursue this idle mode of life, usurp more extensive territories than, with a reasonable share of labor, they would have occasion for ; and have, therefore, no reason to complain if other nations, more industrious and too closely confined, come to take possession of a part of those lands."—(§ 81.)

" It is asked whether a nation may lawfully take possession of some part of a vast country, in which there are none but erratic nations, whose scanty population is incapable of occupying the whole. We have already observed, (§ 81,) in establishing the obligation to cultivate the earth, that those nations cannot exclusively appropriate to themselves more land than they have occasion for, or more than they are able to settle and cultivate. Their unsettled habitation in those immense regions cannot be accounted a true and legal possession ; and the people of Europe, too closely pent up at home, finding land of which the savages stood in no particular need, and of which they made no actual and constant use, were lawfully entitled to take possession of it, and settle it with colonies."—(§ 209.)

This rule of prior discovery, occupation, and of extension by contiguity, to the exclusion of others, has been recognised, with more or less of precision in its application, by all the Europeans who have established themselves in America, and pervades the discussions, negotiations, and treaties, which expressly regulate, or which have *motived*, the limits of their respective territories. So far as regards themselves, and their mutual relations, its chief defect is its vagueness, and the consequent conflict of pretensions, which it either creates, or at least does not prevent.

In its application to the primitive inhabitants of the New World, it is more questionable in use, and more injurious in its effects. When it began to be applied by Spain, Portugal, England, and other European states engaged in colonial enterprises, it was frequently associated with the idea of religion, as exemplified in the bull of Alexander VI defining the rights of Spain and Portugal, and the commission of Henry VII to the Cabots; the concession being to take possession of countries not already occupied by Christians. However defective, therefore, the rule may be in itself, and however destitute of all reason or justice when made the pretext of conquering and reducing to servitude organized communities like those of ancient Peru and Mexico, it is, nevertheless, the real foundation of the great European colonies in America. And these rights of the Indians stand in the way of England, as well as the United States; and cannot be alleged by her against us, and in her own favor. And when a European people has become established in America, and has grown up to national power, the application of the rule is then a matter of absolute necessity ; for the Indian tribes being, for the most part, migratory in their habits, as well as transitory and evanescent in their very existence, and possessing in their barbarous state few or none of the social institutions essential to the preservation of their separate nationality,—to treat them as independent nations, with all the international rights of such, would be absolutely destructive to the civilized states of European stock in or adjoining which they happen to be found, by admitting within the natural limits of such state the intrusion of some other foreign, and perhaps hostile power.

Accordingly, Chief Justice Marshall says:

" All the nations of Europe who have acquired territory on this continent, have asserted in themselves, and have recognised in others, the exclusive right of the discoverer to appropriate the lands occupied by the Indians."

And Judge Story says :

"It may be asked, what was the effect of this principle of discovery, in respect to the rights of the natives themselves? In the view of the Europeans, it created a pecular relation between themselves and the aboriginal inhabitants. The latter were admitted to possess a present right of occupancy, or use in the soil, which was subordinate to the ultimate dominion of the discoverer. * * * *. But, notwithstanding this occupancy, the European discoverers claimed and exercised the right to grant the soil, while yet in the possession of the natives—subject, however, to their right of occupancy; and the title so granted was universally admitted to convey a sufficient title in the soil to the grantees in perfect dominion."

And Chancellor Kent says :

" This assumed but qualified dominion over the Indian tribes, regarding them as enjoying no higher title to the soil than that founded on simple occupancy, and to be incompetent to transfer their title to any other power than the Government which claims the jurisdiction of their territory by right of discovery, arose, in a great degree, from the necessity of the case. * * * It was founded on the pretension of converting the discovery of the country into a conquest; and it is now too late to draw into discussion the validity of that pretension, or the restrictions which it imposes. It is established by numerous compacts, treaties, laws, and ordinances, and founded in immemorial usage. The country has been colonized and settled, and is now held by that title. It is the law of the land, and no court of justice can permit the right to be disturbed by speculative reasonings or abstract rights."

And the peculiar necessity of adhering to the rule, in all dealings between the United States and any of the European Powers, is forcibly illustrated by the pretensions brought forward by Great Britain at Ghent, and the answer of the American ministers, as in the following extracts from one of their letters:

" No maxim of public law has hitherto been more universally established among the powers of Europe possessing territories in America, and there is none to which Great Britain has more uniformly and inflexibly adhered, than that of suffering no interposition of a foreign power in the relations between the acknowledged sovereign of the territory and the Indians situated upon it. Without the admission of this principle, there would be no intelligible meaning attached to stipulation establishing boundaries between the dominions in America of civilized nations possessing territories inhabited by Indian tribes.

* * * " The Indians residing within the limits of the United States * * are so far dependent, as not to have the right to dispose of their lands to any private persons, nor to any power other than the United States, and to be under their protection alone, and not under that of any other power. Whether called subjects, or by whatever name designated, such is the relation between them and the United States. * * * These principles have been uniformly recognised by the Indians themselves * * * in all the * * * treaties between them and the United States.

" The United States cannot consent that Indians residing within their boundaries, as acknowledged by Great Britain, shall be included in the treaty of peace, in any manner which will recognise them as independent nations, whom Great Britain, having obtained this recognition, would hereafter have the right to consider, in every respect, as such. Thus, to recognise those Indians as independent and sovereign nations, would take from the United States, and transfer to those Indians, all the rights of soil and sovereignty over the territory which they inhabit; and this being accomplished through the agency of Great Britain, would place them effectually and exclusively under her protection, instead of being, as heretofore, under that of the United States.

" The United States claim, of right, with respect to all European nations, and particularly with respect to Great Britain, the entire sovereignty over the whole territory, and all the persons embraced within the boundaries of their dominions. Great Britain has no right to take cognizance of the relation subsisting between the several communities or persons living therein; they form, as to her, only parts of the dominion of the United States; and it is altogether immaterial whether, or how far, under their political institutions or policy, these communities or persons are independent states, allies, or subjects. With respect to her, and all other foreign nations, they are parts of a whole, of which the United States are sole and absolute sovereigns."

Recurring, then, to the rule of discovery and occupation in its actual practice, and for the sake of greater pertinency as well as brevity, taking examples in the practice of England herself alone, we find that the English Government, having made discoveries on the Atlantic coast, proceeded to occupy, at detached points on the coast, in right of that discovery, and by the rule of discovery and occupation, and of extension by contiguity, to claim and to grant, *from sea to sea, across the whole continent*, as exemplified in the charters of Massachusetts Bay, Connecticut, and Virginia; and this not only in those early ages, but at the present time; for in right of discovery and occupation in Hudson's bay, she has claimed of us since the treaty of Ghent, and we have conceded to her, an extension by contiguity, through the far interior of the continent, to the foot of the Rocky mountains.

And it follows irresistibly from the premises, that the United States, having in themselves, and as the successors of Spain, all the rights appertaining to the first navigation along the northwest coast, the first discovery of the bay of Juan de Fuca, and of the rivers of Aguilar and Columbia, the first exploration of the same, and the first occupation or settlement of either; and having, in like manner, all the rights of extension across to or along the Pacific, by contiguity, which appertained to Spain as the possessor of New Spain, to England prior to the treaty of Versailles, and to France as the possessor of Louisiana,—it follows irresistibly that we have the right of dominion to the territory of Oregon, wholly exclusive of Great Britain.

Precisely the same conclusion may be reached in a different way, by considering separately the Spanish, the French, and the American title; which, moreover, will be the most convenient means of examining the pretensions of Great Britain.

The Spanish title:

Spain (or her successor, the Mexican-republic) has rights, acknowledged by all the world, as far north on the Pacific as the 42d parallel. And in the same right that she goes thus far, she might, but for the intervention of treaties, go further. Certain it is. that she first explored the northwest coast, by ships from Manilla or Mexico. She is the admitted discoverer of the river of Aguilar, and of the inlet of the Columbia. She discovered the strait of Juan de Fuca. She discovered Nootka sound. First of all Europeans, she founded a setttlement on that coast, at the entrance of the strait of Juan de Fuca. And the natural extension of her possessions northward from California, would carry her along until she met some other power having equal or better rights; and, with the exception of the United States, she would encounter none such until she arrived at Prince of Wales island in latitude 54, and at the settlements of Russia. So well founded were these, the rights of Spain, that while, prior to the conclusion of the Florida treaty, Great Britain was accustomed, as against the United States, to assert rights of sovereignty in the northwest, founded on pretended discoveries and purchases from the Indians, afterwards she was constrained to change her ground, as explained by Mr. Gallatin, (*letter of August* 7, 1827,) and to content herself with simply denying our right of exclusive sovereignty, without pretending to any on her own part. In fact, the claim of England, by discovery and occupation, was of the flimsiest kind—resting only upon Drake's voyage, his landing in the bay of Bodega (latitude 38) in 1578, and some pretended purchases by him of the Indians of that neighborhood; that is to say, the discovery of a country long before discovered by the Spaniards, and taken possession of by them, and to this day comprehended within the acknowledged limits of California. As to his purchases of the Indians, that again can avail nothing; for, by the municipal law of every European Government in America, (and of Britain above all, as already seen,) no foreign state can acquire jurisdiction, or even title, by purchase from Indians within the territorial limits of another. If it were otherwise, the rule would be fatal to the claims of Great Britain on the whole north-west coast; for the owners of the ship Columbia made extensive purchases of the Indians, the political benefit of which would enure to the United States. Her new pretensions, or new grounds of cavil, since resorted to by her, depend on the Nootka convention (so called.)

The Nootka convention is a treaty between Spain and Great Britain, signed at the Escurial on the 28th of October, 1790, in conclusion of the dispute occasioned by the seizure of English vessels at Nootka sound by Don Esteban Martinez, as detailed in the appendix to this report.

When the intelligence of that event reached Europe, it came through Spain, who herself gave the first information to the English Government, and accompanied it with the fullest declaration of a pacific purpose, and of her readiness to enter into all proper explanations. But Mr. Pitt haughtily repelled every friendly advance, and appealed at once to the belligerent propensities of Parliament, in behalf of the wounded honor of the nation; demanded and obtained an extraordinary supply of a million sterling, and prepared for war; and thus hurried Spain, who had neither disposition nor readiness for war at that time, into the conclusion of this treaty.

Article 1 stipulates for the restitution of the property of British subjects dispossessed by Martinez.

Article 2 engages to make restitution of, or compensation for, any like seizures which might have been subsequently made.

Article 3 provides that the respective subjects of Spain and Great Britain shall not be disturbed or molested, either in navigating or carrying on their fisheries in the Pacific ocean, or in the South seas, or in landing on the coasts of those seas, in places not already occupied, for the purpose of carrying on their commerce with the natives of the country, or of making settlements there :—*the whole subject, nevertheless, to the restrictions and provisions specified in the three following articles.*

Article 4 guards against contraband trade with the Spanish settlements in America.

Article 5 agrees that, in any settlements to be made by either party, "the subjects of the other shall have free access, and shall carry on their trade without molestation."

Article 6 provides for the free continuance of the fisheries on the east and west coasts and islands of *South* America, south of the occupation of Spain; and concludes, "Provided, that the said respective subjects shall retain the liberty of landing on the coasts and islands so situated, for the purposes of their fishery, and of erecting thereon huts and other temporary buildings, serving only for those purposes."

Great Britain contends that, with the rights of Spain on the northwest coast, the United States necessarily succeeded to the limitations by which those rights were defined, and the obligations under which they were exercised ; and that, by the above convention, all parts of the northwestern coast of America, not already occupied at that time by either of the contracting parties, should thenceforward be equally open to the subjects of both, for all purposes of commerce and settlement, the sovereignty remaining in abeyance ; and that the convention, establishing a new state of things by compact, abrogates the pre-existing rights (if any) appertaining to Spain.

The United States have constantly denied all this.   They say that, even if the British construction of the Nootka convention and of its effects were correct, it would avail nothing ; because, though the United States might not in other respects have a good title as against Spain, they have as against Great Britain ; which title cannot be weakened in the hands of the United States by the Florida treaty, which quiets that of Spain.

But they deny the correctness of the British construction.   The Nootka convention is, on the face of it, a commercial treaty merely, wholly aside from the question of sovereignty and distinct jurisdiction. 'It has a definite general object—the regulation of the fisheries in the Pacific and the South seas, so as neither to exclude England nor injure Spain.   *That* was the point in controversy between the two Governments.   " The enemies of peace have industriously circulated," says the Count of Florida Blanca, "that Spain extends pretensions and rights of sovereignty over *the whole of the South sea*, as far as China ;" whereas, on the contrary, her sole aim was to vindicate her sovereignty on parts of the coast to which, by the law of nations and the recognition of all Europe, she had the established possession, or right of possession. (*Dec. of June 4th, An. Reg.* 1790.) Accordingly, in the debates upon this treaty in Parliament, it was strenuously objected that, being a treaty of commerce, navigation, and fishery, England had gained nothing by it ; but had, on the contrary, submitted to restrictions of sea-rights, which existed before unrestricted.   " In answer to this, Mr. Pitt maintained (*Parl. Hist.* vol. xxviii, p. 1001) that though what this country had gained *consisted* NOT *of new rights*, it certainly did of new advantages.   We had before a right to the southern whale fishery, and a right to navigate and carry on fisheries in the Pacific ocean, and to trade on the coasts of any part of it northwest of America; but that right not only had not been acknowledged, but disputed and resisted; whereas by the convention it was secured to us—a circumstance which, though no new right, was a new advantage." Not a word of a "new right" to establish colonies in America, or of a "new advantage" in the exclusion of territorial sovereignty previously claimed by Spain. On the contrary, Mr. (now Earl) Grey well argued, that the "settlements" of the third article amounted to nothing, since *access* was everywhere left to both the parties; and if England made a settlement in a valley, Spain might erect a fort on the hill overlooking it; which conclusively shows that the right of colonization was never in the contemplation of the treaty. And Mr. Fox argued the same point at great length, and with great force; demonstrating that, before the treaty, England might colonize in the Pacific; but that now she could only settle, (as the phrase is in the third article,) or build huts, (as restricted in the sixth,) for the sole purpose of the fisheries, excluding colonization. (*Parl. Hist.* vol. xxviii.) Add to which, it is only as a commercial treaty that this convention can, upon the principles contended for by Great Britain in other great controversies, be considered in force; for such treaties only were renewed by the treaty between Spain and Great Britain of July, 1814.

In fact, the Nootka convention is obviously impossible to execute, if the word "settlements" is to include colonies, or carry after it any title of dominion; because the express language permits promiscuous and intermixed settlements everywhere, and over the whole face of the country, to the subjects of both parties; and even declares every such settlement, made by either party, common to the other. Or if, as England contends, the convention is but a recognition of the general rights of all nations, then it admits of such promiscuous settlements by all nations; which is wholly incompatible with any idea of sovereignty, but applies well enough to "huts and other temporary buildings" for the fisheries.

In this view of the subject, the United States further say, that, under the convention, the sovereignty is not in abeyance; it remains unchanged; it is left untouched; temporary commercial rights only are, for the time being, regulated; that the question of sovereignty stands upon its former footing; that, when it comes up, the parties are remitted to their pre-existing rights; and that before the convention, and notwithstanding its provisions, the right of sovereignty appertained to Spain as against Great Britain; or, in the words of the Count of Fernan Nuñez, "By the treaties, demarcations, takings of possession, and the most decided acts of sovereignty exercised by the Spaniards, * * * all the coast to the north of western America, on the side of the South sea, as far as beyond what is called Prince William's sound, * * is acknowledged to belong exclusively to Spain." (*Letter of June* 16, 1790.) And the United States will not be debarred from the exercise of the just rights she derives from Spain, when there is nothing set up against her but new and monstrous constructions of a treaty extorted from Spain by what Lord Porchester justly called "unprovoked bullying," and founded not in right, but in power. (*North Am. Rev.*, vol. xxvii.)

The committee proceed to *the French title:*

When Louisiana was acquired by the United States, it was well known, as already suggested, that the limits were not well defined. Indeed, they were defined on neither side, except along the Mississippi. The northern line, by the British possessions, was fixed in 1818. The southeastern and southwestern was fixed by the Florida treaty; and the question remains, how far does it extend west? This was at the time considered a question with Spain alone. Don Pedro Cevallos says: "From this point, (the intersection of the Red river,) the limits which ought to be established on the northern side are doubtful and little known." (*Letter of April* 13, 1805.) And, in the negotiation of the Florida treaty, Don Luis de Onis admitted the same thing, though he affirmed the Spanish title on the Pacific. But, as between France and Great Britain, or Great Britain and the United States, the successor of all the rights of France, the question would seem to be concluded by the treaty of Versailles, already cited, in which Great Britain relinquishes *irrevocably* all pretensions west of the Mississippi. On the footing of the treaty of Utrecht, ratified by our convention of 1818, England may, possibly, by extension of contiguity, carry her possessions from Hudson's bay across to the Pacific, north of latitude 49°; but, by the treaty of Versailles, we possess the same right, and an exclusive one, to carry our territory across the continent south of that line, in the right of France.

It has been objected, that, in the grant of Louisiana to Crozat by Louis XIV, that province is confined to the country drained by the waters emptying in the Mississippi—excluding, by implication, any other country. But Crozat's grant did not cover the whole of Louisiana as it was when ceded to the United States. Crozat's grant was understood as extending no farther north than latitude 42°; the French possessions north of that parallel being a part of New France, or Canada. And New France, as projected in the most authentic maps, did extend to territory drained, or supposed to be drained, by rivers flowing into the Pacific. In 1717 Louis enlarged Louisiana, by adding thereto the country in the latitude of the Illinois. And this extended dimension of Louisiana has been tacitly admitted by Great Britain, who, while herself possessed of Canada, obtained from France, and of the Hudson's bay country, has, by treaty with us, admitted that the northern limit of Louisiana goes up to latitude 49°; she having already, by the treaty of Versailles, debarred herself of all claim south of that line, and west of the Mississippi.

The American title remains to be considered on its particular merits.

Anterior to the Louisiana treaty, our claim rested on Gray's exploration of the river Columbia, the permanent record of which subsists in the name itself; it being one of the applications of the rule of prior discovery, that the exploration of a river gave rights to the country watered by that river,—as exemplified in the claim of the Mississippi *valley* by France, on the ground of the original exploration of the *river* by her subjects; and some such principle being necessary to give integrity and unity of possession to any one power, and to prevent the intermixture of possessions in a territory having a natural completeness of its own. The defects of this claim consisted of the counter-pretensions of France as the possessor of Louisiana, and of Spain as the possessor of Mexico, and as the first visiter of the Columbia and the coast generally. By the conclusion of the Louisiana treaty and the Florida treaty, these defects were cured. To which had then been added the further claims of the United States in their own right, or their title proper, by reason of Lewis and Clark's expedition, and Mr. Astor's establishment of Astoria, recognised by Great Britain as constituting possession, and also right of continued possession, until the title should be definitively adjusted. Though these several claims conflicted with each other originally, they acquired mutual strength in the same hands; as if three persons claim the same estate—one by deed or devise, another by inheritance, and a third by possession—the union of all in one person, by purchase or otherwise, would result in the best of titles. Thus much, treating it as a dominion founded on discovery and exploration, and partial occupation.

But, in another point of view, this combination of titles becomes yet more important. Having planted her foot on the shore of Hudson's bay, Great Britain claims, against all the world, that she may stretch the other to the Rocky mountains; and the claim is admitted by the rest of the world. Nay, it is from Hudson's bay that her establishments have extended across the continent. Sir Alexander Mackenzie led the way in 1793, and the Northwest Company and the Hudson's Bay Company followed in it, until they had gradually intruded themselves into the valley of the Columbia— not from the Pacific, but proceeding from the Atlantic; and the civil jurisdiction of the British subjects dwelling beyond the Rocky mountains depends this day in *the courts of Upper Canada, by the acts of Parliament of* 43 Geo. III, ch. 131; and 1 and 2 Geo. IV, ch. 66. Which is in conformity with the fact hereinbefore stated, that, prior to the treaty of Versailles, the English Government claimed and granted to the Pacific, by virtue of her possessions in New England and Virginia.

And a pretension of this nature, however extravagant it may seem at the first blush, grows out of the necessities of self-preservation. Great Britain, when she gained a lodgment on the coast of the Atlantic, readily saw, and her colonies soon learned by disastrous experience, how dangerous it would be to them to have a hostile foreign power establish itself behind them. For the same reason that it was important to the British colonies to exclude, if they might, any power from taking possession in their rear, it was important to the French colonies on the Mississippi to prevent any other power from establishing itself in their own rear. Hence they claimed (and rightfully, according to the received law of nations) to have the exclusive dominion, and the right of excluding the entrance of any foreign colonization westward of them, until they should reach some other European power having a better title than theirs; and west of them there was none such, except Spain.

And the precise extent of prolongation by contiguity, to which an actual settlement gives right, must have some relation to the magnitude and population of that settlement, and to the facility with which adjoining vacant lands may promise to be occupied and cultivated by such a population, as compared with any to come from elsewhere; and this, in addition to the considerations of national security.

Important as these principles were to the infant colonies of France and Britain, and strong as are the claims of this nature we derive from the treaties of those two powers, those principles are yet more important, and those claims stronger, in reference to the existing state of North America, and our own position as the leading power of this continent. Who shall undertake to define the limits of the expansibility of the population of the United States? Does it not now flow westward with the never-ceasing advance of a rising tide of the sea? Along a line of more than a thousand miles from the Lakes to the Gulf of Mexico, perpetually moves forward the western frontier of the United States. Here, stretched along the whole

2

length of this line, is the vanguard, as it were, of the onward march of the Anglo-American race, advancing, it has been calculated, at the average rate of about half a degree of longitude each succeeding year. Occasionally, an obstacle presents itself in some unproductive region of country, or some Indian tribe; the column is checked; its wings incline towards each other; it breaks; but it speedily reunites again beyond the obstacle, and resumes its forward progress, ever facing, and approaching nearer and nearer to, the remotest regions of the west. This movement goes on with the predestined certainty and the unerring precision of the great works of eternal Providence, rather than as an act of feeble man. Another generation may see the settlements of our people diffused over the Pacific slope of the Rocky mountains. It is idle to suppose any new colony to be sent out from Great Britain will or can establish itself in the far west, ultimately to stand in competition with this great movement of the population and power of the United States. Nor should any attempt at such competition be countenanced by us. For if the safety of the few thousands of British settlers on the Atlantic, or of French settlers on the Mississippi, required the extension of their exclusive sovereignty to a certain degree west, how far shall that extension not be demanded for the safety of the millions of the United States, who already occupy in full and undisputed sovereignty, and overspread with their teeming population, and unite in the bonds of one great and glorious political society, the whole of the vast valley of the Mississippi and the Missouri?

At a contingency the most delicate in the affairs of this continent, Mr. Monroe issued his celebrated declaration, that while the United States continued neutral and impartial in the contests of the European powers among themselves, it was otherwise in regard to their movements in this hemisphere; that the United States would consider an attempt on their part to extend their peculiar political systems to any part of the New World as dangerous to our peace and safety; and that we could not view a voluntary interposition of theirs in the affairs of the new republics of America with indifference, or in any other light than as the manifestation of an unfriendly disposition towards the United States. (*Message, December* 2, 1823.)

This declaration, it is well known, had the most important immediate effects at the time of its utterance, when certain of the European powers contemplated a forcible interference in the affairs of the Spanish colonies in America. It has deservedly come to be regarded as an essential component part of the international law of the New World. (*Wheaton's Inter. Law, p.* 88.) And great as the force of it is, when applied to the precise case which called for it, still greater is it when considered in its application to the case of an attempt on the part of any European power to found new colonies in North America in parts not yet occupied. It has been the happy fortune of the United States to free itself, by the purchase of Louisiana and Florida, from the presence of European colonies on our southern and western frontiers. The possessions of Great Britain now overhang the United States along their vast northern frontier from the Atlantic to the Pacific. South of that line, the whole continent, from the great lakes to the Isthmus of Darien, is occupied by Americans, by children of the soil, by governments independent of Europe. And it is due alike to our highest interests and to our honor to have it universally understood, that neither Great Britain, nor any other European power, is any longer to consider the unsettled parts of the continent, adjoining the settlements of the United States, in the nature of unoccupied lands for the reception of European colonies. If Great Britain had any pretext to claim the Territory of Oregon as a part of her possessions on the lakes, of her existing colonies, it would be otherwise. But she does not. She distinctly puts her claim to Oregon on the ground that it is unoccupied territory, just like Virginia or Massachusetts before she colonized them; and that, as unoccupied savage territory, she may now colonize the Columbia river ;—not that it is part of a colony now possessed by her, but country in which she has the right at this day to found a new colony.

"Great Britain considered the whole of the unoccupied parts of America as being open to her future settlements, as heretofore. They included within these parts, as well that portion of the northwest coast lying between the 42d and 51st degrees of latitude, as any other parts. The principle of colonization on that coast, or els where, on any portions of those continents not yet occupied, Great Britain was not prepared to relinquish."—*Mr. Rush's letter, August 12,* 1824.

This pretension the committee deem to be inadmissible, and prejudicial to the rights, the security, and the peace of the United States.

There is a class of reasons applicable to this point, which is every day acquiring more and more force. It is the situation of the Indians in the interior of the continent. It has at all times been the policy of Great Britain —a policy little in keeping with her ostentation of humanity in regard to the black race—to keep the red men under subsidy to her, so as to have them always ready to bring into the field against the United States. At the epoch of the Revolution, we proposed that the Indians should be suffered to remain neutral; but England refused. She has kept them under arms, or in a semi-hostile state, against us, more or less constantly, from that day to this. Our commissioners at Ghent proposed an agreement for the perpetual neutrality of the Indians; but England again refused it. The perseverance of Great Britain in this policy has been deplorably injurious to us; and its effects are written with the scalping knife and the brand of the Indian, in letters of blood and fire, in the history of the southern and western States. And this, the unholy policy of Great Britain in regard to the Indians, has done more than any and every other cause united, to waste, degrade, and barbarize them, so as to render them a curse alike to us and to themselves. By the acquisition of Florida, the influence of the British over the Indians of the United States was shut out from the south ; but it still operates unchecked, and is fostered and kept alive, by regular Government subsidies in the northwest ; and is exerted without any counteraction among the Indians of the remote west, and will continue to be exerted, in all respects to our loss and injury, until the Hudson's Bay Company is expelled from the territory of Oregon, and it is possessed in full and indisputed sovereignty by the United States.

In conclusion of this branch of their instructions, it only remains for the committee to advert to certain particular facts in the present political relations of the territory of Oregon, confirmatory of, and connected with, the general considerations they have suggested.

Great Britain had very much distinguished herself at an early period, by voyages of discovery in the seas to the northeast of this continent. Thus it happened that she acquired territorial rights on the shores of Hudson's bay, which at the congress of Utrecht were formally acknowledged by France, as before stated. The extent of this territory was not then, nor until long afterwards, definitively settled. Meanwhile, among the corrupt monopolies of the reign of Charles II, was the grant of a charter to the

"Adventurers of the Hudson's Bay Company." Their declared and proper objects were, of course, navigation, and trade in the furs, fish, or other productions of Hudson's bay. *Exploration* was, indeed, one of the benefits anticipated from the company ; but the company itself proved, for more than a century, to be the great obstacle to exploration ; or, in the emphatic language of the London Quarterly Review, (a competent witness on such a point,) "From the moment this body of 'adventurers' was instituted, the *spirit* of 'adventure' died away; and every succeeding effort was palsied by the baneful influence of a monopoly, of which the discovery of a northwest passage was deemed the forerunner of destruction." This company is to America, precisely what the East India Company is to Asia. It has been suffered to extend its power from Labrador southwestwardly to Lake Superior, thence along the *ligne des versants* of the Mississippi and the Missouri, and so sweeping around by the base of the Rocky mountains to the Slave Lake, and thence back to the extreme northeastern shores of the Atlantic. A glance at the map will show the vast extent of these imperial dominions. (*Bouchette's Br. Dom. vol.* 1, *p.* 32.) When, by the aid of the Anglo-American provinces, Great Britain had subdued Canada, this did not become incorporated with the possessions of the Hudson's Bay Company. On the contrary, when the independence of the United States gave rise to new relations in the northwest, the Hudson's Bay Company was placed by Britain on the footing of an independent power ; and in regulating the rights of mutual transit in that quarter, Jay's treaty contains this clause : "the country within the limits of the Hudson's Bay Company only excepted." That is to say, when the territorial or commercial rights of the United States are to be restricted, the Hudson's Bay company is put forward as an independent foreign state. So also is it when there is opportunity or occasion to extend British rights in competition with ours ; as in dealings with the Indians it has repeatedly happened, where the acts of the company have at all times been greatly injurious to the United States. But, on the contrary, if the United States, or any other power, seeks to repress the pretensions of the company, it is no longer left by Great Britain to stand on its own bottom as a political community, but is taken under the wing of the British Government. This, indeed, we know is the precise mode in which the East India Company has been made the instrument of conquering the hundred millions of Hindostan.

After the Hudson's Bay Company had, for a length of time, lorded it in sole supremacy over the Indians of the extensive region claimed by it, there sprung up a competitor of its profitable fur trade, in the Northwest Company of Montreal. These two companies did not scrup e to engage in continual feuds, growing out of jealousies of trade, and mutual complaints of violated privileges; nay, they actually waged hostilities one against the other, in the guise of sovereign States—rendering the interior of the continent a scene of rapine, outrage, and bloodshed. (*Earl of Selkirk, Claims, &c.*)

These empire-companies, and their traders, trappers, and agents, have been the immediate instruments of much of that perpetual intermeddling of Great Britain with the Indians of the United States, which, from 1775 to the present day, has never ceased to be practised to our injury ; and the fruits of which were seen in every one of the disasters of the west and northwest, from the massacres of Wyoming and Cherry Valley, and the defeats of Harmar and St. Clair, to the later enterprises of Tecumseh and of Black Hawk.

This latter company (the Northwest Company, so called) it was, which fraudulently obtained possession of Astoria in 1812, and hoisted the British flag on the Columbia. (*Irving's Astoria.*) Its differences with the Hudson's Bay Company were at length adjusted. In 1821 the two companies became one—continuing to act under the charter of the Hudson's Bay Company; and, by act of Parliament, the company received a grant of civil jurisdiction, which it now exercises at all its establishments. That is, the Hudson's Bay Company is the medium through which Great Britain exercises exclusive civil jurisdiction over all the territory of Oregon, in which it is conceded, on all hands, our rights are at least equal to hers. Nor civil jurisdiction only. It is known by the official report of Mr. Slacum, who recently visited the territory in behalf of the United States, that the company has, in addition to a number of minor factories, one at Vancouver, on the Columbia, which is in all respects a military post, though, like the sepoys and other troops of Hindostan, the garrison consists of the servants of the company—not of officers and men bearing the Queen's commission. Of other establishments of the company, (which are in name, as in fact, forts,) there are known to be Fort Umqua, on the Umqua; Fort George, Fort Nez Percés, Fort Okanagan, Fort Colville, and Koolante fort; besides Fort Vancouver, on the Columbia, or its branches; and Fort Nasqually, south of the strait of Juan de Fuca.

To prove these general facts, and also to show the effect of them, a few authentic statements follow, from persons of approved authority.

The President's message, of the 23d of December, 1837, contains this information:

"The Hudson's Bay Company have also several depots, situated on water-courses, in the interior of the country; the principal one is at Fort Vancouver, on the northern bank of the Columbia river, about eighty or one hundred miles from its mouth. It is known, by information recently obtained, that the English company have a steamboat on this river, and that they have a saw-mill, and are cutting timber on the territory claimed by the United States, and are shipping it in considerable quantities to the Sandwich islands."

Mr. Cambreleng, in a letter to Mr. Benton of the 12th January, 1829, says:

"I have in my possession the actual returns of the furs collected by the Hudson's Bay Company for the year 1828, which, according to a valuation made by one who has a thorough knowledge of the trade, amount to $894,879 85. The shares of that company have increased from £60, or 40 per cent. below par, to £240 sterling, or 140 per cent. above par. The business of the company has continued to increase at the rate of from $60,000 to $100,000 annually. The prosperous condition of the Hudson's Bay Company may be attributed, in some measure, to the advantages enjoyed by the British traders, who procure their manufactures without duty, while the American traders pay 40 per cent. and upwards; and who can send their furs to the American market, while our traders pay a duty in the British market. But the most important advantage enjoyed by the Hudson's Bay Company, is the admirable harbor at the mouth of the Columbia, which we virtually and unfortunately granted them by our treaty of 1818. That settlement at the mouth of the Columbia river is now the centre of an immense trade in furs, and, unless we take some steps to place our traders on an equal footing with the British, and secure to the former the privilege of trading in safety within our own dominions at least, our Indian trade must decline, and we must make up our minds to surrender the whole Indian country to Great Britain."—*Sen. Doc. 1828-'29, No. 67.*

Mr. Irving says:

"Though the [Hudson's Bay] Company, by treaty, have a right to a participation only in the trade of these regions, [beyond the Rocky mountains,] and are, in fact, but tenants in sufferance; yet have they quietly availed themselves of the original oversight, and subsequent supineness of the American Government, to establish a monopoly of the trade of the river [Columbia] and its dependencies ; and are adroitly proceeding to fortify themselves in their usurpation, by securing all the strong points of the country.

" Nor is it likely the latter [the American traders] will ever be able to maintain any footing in the land, until the question of territorial right is adjusted between the two countries. The sooner that takes place, the better. It is a question too serious to national pride, if not to national interest, to be slurred over; and every year is adding to the difficulties which environ it.

" he resources of the country * * in the hands of America, enjoying a direct trade with the East Indies, would be brought into quickening activity, and might soon realize the dream of Mr. Astor, in giving rise to a flourishing commercial empire."—*Rocky Mountains, vol.* 2.

The plans of Great Britain in respect to this country are shadowed forth by Sir Alexander Mackenzie as follows:

" But, whatever course may be taken from the Atlantic, the Columbia is the line of communication from the Pacific ocean pointed out by nature, as it is the only navigable river in the whole extent of Vancouver's minute survey of that coast. Its banks, also, form the first level country in all the southern extent of continental coast from Cook's entry, and, consequently, the most northern situation fit for colonization, and suitable for the residence of a civilized people. By opening this intercourse between the Atlantic and Pacific oceans, and forming regular establishments through the interior, and at both extremes, as well as along the coasts and islands, the entire command of the fur trade of North America might be obtained from latitude 48 degrees north to the pole—except that portion of it which the Russians have in the Pacific. To this may be added the fishery in both seas, and the markets of the four quarters of the globe. Such would be the field for commercial enterprise ; and incalculable would be the produce of it, when supported by the operations of that credit and capital which Great Britain so pre-eminently possesses."—*Travels, vol.* 2.

To which the same writer adds, that the effect of the development of those plans would be the complete exclusion of Americans from the country, and the most important political as well as commercial advantages to the United Kingdom.

The committee will have occasion to submit to the House additional information on these points, when they dispose of that part of their instructions which refers to the statistical condition and political value of the country of Oregon. It is sufficient for the immediate purpose to have demonstrated that the plan of the British to put an end to American enterprise in the valley of the Columbia has succeeded.

Still, this object has been accomplished under the shelter of a convention, which provides that the country of Oregon, together with its harbors, bays, and creeks, and the navigation of all rivers within the same, shall, for the time being, be free and open to the vessels, citizens, and subjects of the two powers; and which thus professes to give equal present advantages to the people of each nation, and to prejudge the ultimate rights of neither. But the practical effect of the convention is the reverse, in that nearly all the present advantages are enjoyed by England, and the ultimate rights of the United States are seriously endangered.

This arises from the peculiar organization of the Hudson's Bay Company, which now in fact rules over the whole country, and has exclusive possession of its trade—just as completely as the East India Company in Hindostan at the period of its early conquests there, when it was a close corporation, and independent of the control of the King's ministers. Individual traders, and ordinary commercial companies, cannot stand against it. They cannot compete in resources with this great empire-corporation. Besides which, a powerful incorporated company like this, having exclusive privileges of trade by charter, and those privileges conveying *territory* as appurtenant to trade—a monster and an anomaly in its nature as it is,—such a company is in itself, to all intents and purposes, a territorial government. It has all the civil and all the military machinery of government. Nay, more. The acts of Parliament already referred to give to the courts of

Upper Canada the same civil jurisdiction, in all respects, within the parts of America not within the limits of Lower or Upper Canada, nor of any civil government of the United States, as they have within the limits of Upper Canada. England may appoint justices of the peace, or constitute other inferior courts in those parts. There is no provision in the act to except citizens of the United States, or country claimed by the United States, from this jurisdiction. And these provisions are precisely applicable to the country beyond the Rocky mountains, and to that only; and there is no other part of America to which they do apply. This, indeed, is well understood by American citizens in Oregon to be the fact, as the committee have been expressly informed. So that the Hudson's Bay Company not only monopolizes the trade of Oregon, but may control the inhabitants, and even send them to Upper Canada to be tried for imputed offences.

The privileges of the Hudson's Bay Company operate injuriously in another respect. Experience has shown the necessity of military posts among the Indians. The company accordingly has its great post, and its lesser forts—all of them British military posts in fact, but with the peculiarity, that its flag not being the Queen's flag, the Government is enabled to pursue the disingenuous course of claiming rights and territory in virtue of acts performed by it, while in the same breath disavowing all Government responsibility for those acts. But the United States has no military post there. It has no gigantic company, like that of Hudson's Bay, to be put forward to act the ambiguous and insidious part of a government, or of private individuals, as the policy of state may render most convenient. If it establishes a post, it must do so openly and aboveboard, in its own name. But this Great Britain objects to, so that still the monopoly of trade and of civil and military power shall be held by her *indirectly*, through the means of the Hudson's Bay Company.

The committee are of opinion that this ground of distinction ought to be no longer admitted by the United States. So long as Great Britain takes to herself the fruits of the operations of these empire-corporations, and so long as the millions of subjects they conquer, and the vast realms they subdue, are governed and held for her advantage, she ought not to be permitted to set up any distinction, in her dealings with a foreign state, between their acts and hers. So far as regards the rights or the safety of that foreign state, a military post established by the East India Company, or the Hudson's Bay Company, is a military post established by Great Britain. Not to perceive this, is to shut our eyes to the system of operations, by means of which Great Britain has built up the stupendous fabric of her power in the east and the west.

The injustice done to the United States by the double use which Great Britain makes of the Hudson's Bay Company, was strongly urged by Mr. Gallatin, in his conferences with the British ministers on the subject, in 1826 and 1827. The British ministers were not insensible to the force of his objections. And the following passage of Mr. Gallatin's letter of December 20, 1826, is important in its bearing upon the question of what legislation Congress may adopt, without infringement of the treaty relations of the two powers :

"The establishment of a distinct Territorial Government on the west side of the Stony mountains would also be objected to as an attempt to exercise exclusive sovereignty. I observed that, although the Northwest Company might, from its being incorporated, from the habits of the men they employed, and from having a monopoly with respect to trade, so far as British subjects were concerned, carry on a species of government, without the assistance of that of Great Britain, it was otherwise with us. Our population there would consist of several independent companies and individuals. We had always been in the habit, in our most remote settlements, of carrying laws, courts, and justices of the peace with us. There was an absolute necessity, on our part, to have some species of government. Without it, the kind of sovereignty, or rather jurisdiction, which it was intended to admit, could not be exercised on our part. It was suggested, and seemed to be acquiesced in, that the difficulty might be obviated, provided the erection of a new Territory was not confined exclusively to the territory west of the mountains; that it should be defined as embracing all the possessions of the United States west of a line that should be at some distance from, and east of, the Stony mountains."

The committee have reported their bill in precise accordance with these suggestions of Mr. Gallatin, acquiesced in, as he informs us, by the British ministers in 1826. They have accompanied it only with such suggestions and arguments as seemed indispensably necessary to its support—retaining the right hereafter to present, if they should think it necessary, a more full and satisfactory report on all the facts and considerations bearing on this great and important subject.

The portrait of Aaron Venable Brown was graciously furnished
by the Tennessee State Library and Archives, Nashville,
Tennessee, to which source we here give our thanks.

This is the twelfth booklet of western history to come from
Ye Galleon Press.

Of this edition 500 *copies were printed.*

This is copy No. 116 .